A SUPERNATURAL CONDITION

SPIRITS, ALIENS AND THE AFTERLIFE

Diana Formisano Willett

authorHOUSE®

AuthorHouse™
1663 Liberty Drive
Bloomington, IN 47403
www.authorhouse.com
Phone: 1 (800) 839-8640

Published by AuthorHouse 02/26/2016

ISBN: 978-1-5049-7970-2 (sc)
ISBN: 978-1-5049-7969-6 (hc)
ISBN: 978-1-5049-7971-9 (e)

Library of Congress Control Number: 2016903107

Print information available on the last page.

Any people depicted in stock imagery provided by Thinkstock are models, and such images are being used for illustrative purposes only.
Certain stock imagery © Thinkstock.

This book is printed on acid-free paper.

CONTENTS

The Metaphysical

Life never ends. Life continues forever in different dimensions and in different forms.

—James Van Praagh, *Ghosts Among Us*

Spirits are metaphysical and are also considered transcendental in nature. The existence of apparitions, ghosts, and orbs that contain spirits has not been verified yet. Because these apparitions and ghosts are lacking in reality, they are considered to be the supernatural. Ghosts are created when the spirit of a person who has died remains connected to this world because it is attached to it through unfinished business or just an unwillingness to move on. A ghost that does not move on to the next realm may eventually become a vengeful spirit, poltergeist, or part of a subclass of vengeful spirits called specters.

The supernatural is defined as "not existing in nature or subject to explanation according to natural laws; not physical or material." The supernatural is also considered the occult (Free Dictionary by Farlex, s.v. "supernatural"). When dealing with the occult, you must be very careful. You may encounter supernatural beings, which are incorporeal beings believed to have powers to affect the course of human events. Watch out for orbs when dealing with the supernatural. Orbs are often seen in locations where some form of paranormal activity is taking place. I have pictures of white orbs seen in my house. A white orb indicates that the spirit is trapped on this plane. The spirit whose orb is white also indicates that the spirit is here to offer protection to the people in the area. White energy is usually perceived as highly positive in nature.

I verify the existence of spirits and orbs by means of the photographs I have included in this book. As seen below (image 1), you can see faces on the video from the camera in my living room.

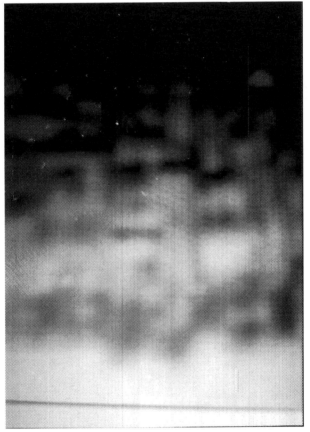

Image 1. These images are spirits coming out of an enormous white orb. There are numerous spirits in this photo. I can see my dead mother-in-law but do not recognize anyone else.

In Image 2, you can see the spirit exiting the orb. The spirit image is seen through the mirror. You can also see numerous spirit faces in these photos.

Image 2. Look at the scary face coming out of this gigantic orb. This is the portal.

Image 3. Look at the numerous spirit faces along the walls.

In images 2 and 3, you can definitely see a large orb and a spirit face emanating from the orb in the mirror images. This face looks rather scary. It may be the spirit of my mother-in-law coming out of the orb. I spoke to a psychic in September 2015 and he believes these spirits, which are entering my house along with my husband's spirit, are trying to help him cross over and resolve any unfinished business.

So what is unfinished business when you die? It's the concerns of the dying patient that require some sort of resolution before death that the patient will accept. This unfinished business seems to drive the dead to haunt. The spirit will remain here on earth, which would account for many apparitions and ghost sightings. If the death is sudden and unexpected, some spirits will remain at or near the site of death. The spirit will stay behind to take care of unfinished business.

When we die, we usually default to heaven. No one will automatically become a ghost. These so-called ghosts that decide to stay on earth after death feel they have some type of unfinished business here. The importance of the unfinished business is determined by the person experiencing it.

In images 4 and 5, you can see a picture of my dead husband carrying some type of object in the driveway. It looks like a hair dryer to me. I don't know why he is in the driveway, but it has to do with the unfinished business that draws him back here.

Image 4. My dead husband visiting. This image was on my security camera.

Image 5. My dead husband holding what looks like a hair dryer.

There are many reasons why the dead return because of unfinished business. Some of these reasons may include to ask forgiveness, to settle unfinished business and return in dreams, to serve as guides and angels, to give health warnings, to deliver messages, to prepare us for death, to show us their realm, to come as guardians and guides, or to seek guidance from us.

Let's talk about the dead seeking forgiveness. This is part of the unfinished business I will be discussing in this book.

I know my husband comes back seeking forgiveness because he has appeared in my bedroom crying. I once woke up around three o'clock in the morning in my bed and happened to look toward my dresser. I saw my husband standing near the side of the bed where he used to sleep. He smiled at me, and I was not afraid at the time. I didn't move and just continued to lie in my bed. I was watching him and couldn't believe what I was seeing.

He stood near the side of the bed and looked at my nail polishes and then at the floor. He was smiling at this time, looking down at where his BiPAP machine used to be. A BiPAP stands for a bilevel positive airway pressure.

This machine is a management tool for chronic obstructive pulmonary disease and acute and chronic respiratory failure. My dead husband then started to look at the clothes in my closet and smiled. I didn't say anything, and all of a sudden he moved to the middle of the bed area and started to sob. I had never heard anyone sob like that. He then disappeared. This scared me, and now I am afraid every night this will happen again. I'm sure he feels quite bad about dying and leaving me and my son. He also brings other spirits here, as I've documented in the photos included in this book.

The way to communicate with a spirit, if you want to do it yourself and not seek the help of a medium, is to raise your vibrational rate. Your vibrational rate is your energy state. Our thoughts, our physical health, our emotions, and our beliefs all contribute to our vibrational rates. Everything in the universe is made up of energy vibrating at different frequencies. Even solid objects are made up of vibrational energy fields, including you. Vibrations will operate at either a high or low frequency, and this is also true for the vibrations that occur within our own beings. Lower vibration rates are associated with poor health, negative emotions and thoughts, and lack of spiritual awareness. On the other hand, higher vibrational rates are associated with positive thinking and emotions, good health, and a strong spiritual awareness.

Sometimes you may experience vibes from another person. When this happens, you are tapping into their energy—the vibrational rate of that person. By eating correctly and eliminating drugs, alcohol, refined foods, and smoking from your life, you can increase your vibrational rate. Eat fresh fruits and vegetables and whole grains, and if you can, try to buy organic foods as much as possible.

By helping others, you will automatically increase your vibrational rate. Also try to meditate and quiet your mind. Exercising, listening to music (which I love to do), and maybe even volunteering will also help. Anything that brings you joy will raise your vibrational rate. By doing all of these things, you can then communicate with the spirits. Of course, if you are afraid to communicate with a spirit or spirits, do not attempt to do this.

I am sometimes afraid to communicate with the dead. They are not the same as they were when living here on earth. Their reactions and what they may do are quite concerning. Look at images 1, 2, and 3. The image that looks like my mother-in-law could be her, but her spirit is different when dead. I feel no urge to communicate with her.

Now let's talk about spirits returning in your dreams and why they communicate this way.

When we dream, we are already in the astral planes, thus making it easier for the dead to communicate with us. When dreaming, the dormant, logical brain is less likely to jump in and stop communication of a paranormal kind. The dead will communicate in dreams, and you can see they are happy or mad at you for what you are doing here on earth. I have had upsetting dreams and happy dreams about my husband. The spirit can hear and see what you are doing and also communicate displeasure or joy in your dreams. The spirits have free choice and will visit the places where they had happiness and joy. The dead can even foreshadow the future.

My son tells me about dreams he has of his father and other people. My son saw a little girl with pigtails sitting on my couch in the living room and reading a magazine while he was dreaming. His father tries to communicate with him in dreams. My husband will appear angry in my son's dreams. Even in my dreams, my husband does not appear at peace but very angry and disturbed. I spoke to a psychic, and he feels my husband will appear as different people to upset us. He has a good side and a bad side.

While sleeping one night, I awoke and saw three toy soldiers standing right by my bed. They were gray, with no real color at all, and they were looking at me with an angry glare. I woke up and started screaming, and they immediately disappeared. This was just the beginning of more apparitions in 2015 which I will discuss in the next chapter on spirits.

The next reason for the dead returning is to serve as guides and angels.

We do not walk alone in this life! With you walks your most loyal friends—your spirit guide and angels. Your guardian or (gatekeeper) spirit guide is always with you. This soul has been with you since day one of this earthly life and is here to protect and guide you. This is truly the case, as my spirit guide saved me from drowning at the age of ten.

When I was ten, I went to a private pool with friends. My mother was working, and my father was sleeping because he worked the night shift at a hospital in the Bronx. I went with these kids but told the older one that I did not know how to swim. He said that was okay and put me on his shoulders and started to walk around the pool. All of a sudden, someone from behind pushed him, and I fell off his shoulders and landed at the bottom of the pool. I immediately turned around and saw a gigantic white hand come down into the water. I looked at it for a second, and it gestured for me to come toward it. I grabbed the hand, and it immediately grabbed my hand and pulled me up to the top of the pool. It pulled me up with such force that I had to close my eyes because the water was gushing in my face.

I then saw the boy who had been holding me on his shoulders, and he said he had not pulled me up from the water. He said everyone was looking for me, and they did not know where I was. Well, I went home and told my parents what happened, and my mother told me it had been my guardian angel that saved me. I will never forget this. A priest told me I was blessed.

Before you incarnate on earth, you pick the guide that will be most suitable for you and the life you will encounter. They know your energy, thoughts, and emotions. They do not judge you but are there to guide and help you along your journey.

I did see some type of spirit guide or angel once in my bedroom. I was by myself in my room and was watching television. I happened to look to the right and saw this entity appearing in the air. It looked medieval, which means it was from the Middle Ages or was some type of archangel from centuries ago. Archangel Michael's aura color is purple, and this entity was dressed in purple. I am not saying this was Archangel Michael, but it was some type of spirit guide or angel from long ago. It was wearing a purple cloth and was looking straight ahead. Then, all of a sudden, it smiled. I could see the eyes very well at that time, and the thoughts it projected said, "I know everything about you, and I was there in the water protecting you."

This entity used what is called telepathy to communicate with me. Telepathy is accurately reading the thoughts of others. Sigmund Freud believed telepathy was possible when he noticed that analysts and their patients could pick up on each other's thoughts. Some people may experience telepathy on occasion, and others may be able to turn this ability on and off.

This entity then immediately disappeared. I will never forget that face. It did look like a spirit, and it was small in size. I wish you all could find or see your spirit guide.

What is an angel?

An angel is defined as a messenger, a heavenly envoy.

Angelic hands will also lift and protect you from danger. Heavenly beings are referred to as angels. Angels are divided into three categories:

1. The first sphere is made up of heavenly counselors, including seraphim, cherubim, and thrones.
2. The second sphere is made up of angels that work as heavenly governors, including dominions, virtues, and powers.
3. Finally, the third sphere is made up of angels that function as heavenly messengers, including principalities, archangels, and angels.

The angels we are most familiar with are in the last order. These are the ones that are mostly concerned with human affairs. The ones we all know best are our guardian angels. They are considered our companion angels. As more light and love increases on this planet, your guardian angel will not need to guard you but to guide you.

Beyond the angels are the archangels. My archangel's name is Uriel. The four archangels are Gabriel, Michael, Raphael, and Uriel. Beyond the archangels are the principalities. They guide large groups on earth, such as corporations and more of a unified global order in their hearts.

The first order of the second sphere are the powers. They are the keepers of collective history. Beyond the powers are the virtues. They can beam out massive levels of divine energy. The dominions are the heavenly beings that govern the activities of all the heavenly groups of the ones lower than they are.

The first order in the third sphere is the thornes. They are the companion angels of the planet. The earth angel is the guardian of this world. Now beyond the thornes are the cherubim, which are the guardians of light and the stars. This light will filter down from heaven and touch all human beings.

The seraphim is the highest order of angels. These celestial beings are said to surround the throne of God, singing the music of the spheres. I have heard the music of heaven. When my husband died, I was in my bedroom and started hearing music emanating from the ceiling near my window. The music was some type of chimes. I saw a shadow come down from the ceiling while I was hearing this music. I saw a black shadow figure walk to my nightstand and look at the picture of my husband, me, and my son on a cruise ship. It just stood there staring at the picture. It looked like my husband's figure. I did not say a word, and it disappeared. It was an unbelievable thing to see!

The next reason why spirits come back is to give health warnings to the living. When a spirit is present, you will hear a buzzing in the ear. This continuously happens to me and my son. It is a high-frequency sound in the ears. When this happens, look at your surroundings for a message. When a spirit is in the house, we hear a buzzing sound. I have heard this sound while I was at work, and of course, I tried to ignore the communication. I felt that the spirit was making sure I was all right at work and wasn't experiencing any malicious behavior from coworkers.

There are also other signs that a spirit is present, including flickering lights and appliances that switch on and off. This is true, because I experienced this type of communication from my mother. My son at the time was in his playpen, and I went upstairs to get a dish towel out of the closet. All of a sudden, I heard the blender in the kitchen go on. My son screamed and cried, because he was afraid of the sound. I ran downstairs and immediately unplugged the blender. I was amazed and bewildered by how or why this happened. At the time, I was standing in the kitchen near the phone. I looked up and saw the calendar on the wall. It was May 6—the anniversary of my mother's death. So, spirits will communicate in many ways.

Another sign a spirit is present is by a familiar smell, such as perfume or even a cigar. This can definitely indicate a spirit is present. You may see a butterfly or a bird flying around you, which will indicate you are not alone and a loved one is present. Vivid dreams indicate that a spirit is trying to communicate with you. The feeling that someone is watching you indicates love and protection from a spirit. If a particular number is repeated on clocks or even a billboard, it could be an anniversary or a special number.

Spirits can deliver messages several different ways, but the most common type is dream visitations. Deceased loved ones and spirit guides will connect with you in your dreams. Sometimes the deceased loved one will appear in a dream surrounded by some sort of light. This does not necessarily happen all the time. I have dreamed of my husband without a bright light surrounding him. The dead will talk to you in these dreams and either convey messages or tell you they are fine on the other side.

The next reason why the dead return is to prepare us for death. My husband's spirit was flying around the bedroom for two weeks before he died. He told me that he saw me sleeping at night and he was flying around the room. I told him he had just been dreaming, but he said he hadn't been. Spirits were calling his soul to be released from his sick body.

The final reason for the dead returning is to show us their realm.

Isaiah 14:9a says: "The realm of the dead below is all astir to meet you at your coming" (New International Version).

The dead want to guide us to their realm beyond this physical life. When the dying person is ready to pass on, loved ones and even former beloved pets may be the person's soul guide to the other realm. I asked a psychic about my mother, and she told me that my mother was in heaven where there were beautiful yellow flowers. When my husband first died, I used to pass the gift shop at Yale-New Haven Hospital where I worked. I saw these beautiful yellow roses in the window, and I asked a psychic why I was staring at these roses. She replied that my husband wanted me to have them. So, as you can see, the dead *do* communicate with us in all different ways.

The dead may also come as guardians and guides. The terms *angel*, *spirit guide*, and *guardian spirit* refer to beings that help us, guide us, and deliver messages. Seeing these beings often occurs in fleeting encounters.

Guardian spirits can also be spirits of human beings, even though they have not fully evolved spiritually or finished their own incarnations. These guardian spirits will come back because they have a personal interest in protecting you and are interested in your well-being.

A guardian spirit has some sort of connection with you. It could be a decreased family member, a friend who died, or an ancestor you do not know. Image 6 in chapter 2 depicts a woman spirit in the living room. I feel this is an ancestor who is trying to protect me and my son. These guardian spirits could also be someone you knew in a different life. Because this life has many challenges and can be very hard, we are lucky we have this type of help available. Many spirits have incarnated and do not come back as themselves.

I have asked a psychic about my father. She told me my father has reincarnated. I believe this, because he has never come back except one time just after his death. I was coming home from work and went down the subway in New York City to catch the train. I was walking out, and there was an elevator that opened up with other people in it. I happened to glance at the elevator and saw my father in the elevator. He looked down, appearing very sad, and the elevator closed. I told my mother what had happened, and she told me my father missed you. That was the only time I had a connection with him. My mother said my father adored me.

At times, the dead may need our help and seek our guidance. When my husband appeared in my room crying, he was definitely seeking my help and guidance to cross over to the light. Something is keeping him here, and I feel it is guilt. We go to church and pray for his soul to seek peace and happiness. As you can see from this book, it has not happened yet.

CHAPTER 2

APPARITIONS AND SPIRITS

On the 120th day after fertilization of an egg by a sperm, the embryo starts producing waves as it becomes subject to basic influences coming from the cosmic rays. This has been described as "The Angel's blowing the spirit" (From the book Spirit, Man, Jinn by Ahmed Hulusi (Chapter 5-The Human Spirit). At this point, the spirit of the human is created. After day 120, the astral body is being sculpted, so abortion is considered murder. It's at this time when the core of the brain in the embryo starts to produce and sculpt the astral body, which is the personal spirit. Therefore, if something happens to the embryo at this time, this *spirit* carries on to live forever.

Whenever we die and the activity of the brain stops and the electromagnetic force of the physical body has been cut off, the person will feel himself living in a holographic body of light and then carry on living under this influence. This is the state that you return to life in, which is living in the astral body. The astral body still continues to feel the same fears, anxieties, and love that the person felt during his lifetime in the physical body.

The astral body will now reside with the dimension of light, which is still the conscious mind, but it goes through transformations from the biological body into the dimension of the spirit, or the astral body. This dimension of light is the twin of our planet. One day in this realm is equal to one thousand years on earth, which is written in the Koran. The astral body will continue to carry on for eternity.

After death, as discussed earlier, we all retain memories from our previous lives. We remember our loved ones and the pain and emotional upset we felt here on earth. This fact is why the spirit or soul haunts and comes back to seek either forgiveness or helps loved ones here on earth.

How are spirit photographs produced? The camera may serve as some sort of medium device, enabling a spirit to communicate to us or just manifest itself. This photographic sitting could be understood as some sort of séance. Spirits are very unpredictable in their behavior as people. They are able to go from place to place and create havoc if they choose to. I have experienced these destructive behaviors in the house by apparitions and/or ghosts.

A ghost is thought to be the energy, soul, or personality of a person who has died and is for some reason stuck between this plane of existence and the next. Many researchers believe these spirits do not know they are dead.

When my husband first died, I was lying down in my bedroom ready to go to sleep. I had a glass of soda with ice by my nightstand. I was just lying down and all of a sudden heard the sound of ice moving in a glass. I thought it was my glass, but the sound was coming from the door to the bedroom, which was closed. I then felt someone sit on my bed, and I drifted off to sleep. I woke up to a tremendous white light that took up the entire room. It was the brightest light I have ever seen. This light was so bright, in fact, that I was blinded by it. As I tried to see what it was, the light immediately disappeared. This was my husband's spirit. He used to have a rum and coke with ice at night, and I think he did not know he had died. It took some time for him to accept the fact he was dead.

Image 6. You can see an apparition of a woman near the door. Who she is, and why is she there? I can't answer those questions.

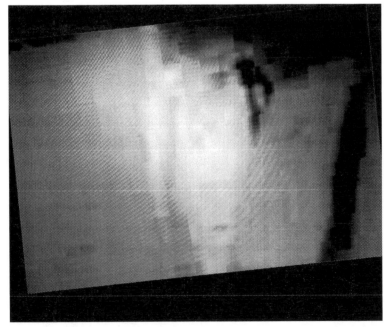

Image 7. There are about three ghost faces here. I hope you can see them.

Image 8. This is a photo of a gigantic orb moving outside with numerous spirits traveling in it. It appeared gray color on the camera. A gray or white orb depicts a guardian angel that is near you.

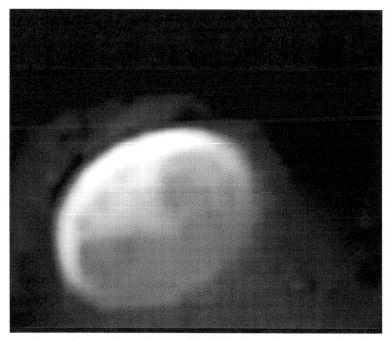

Image 9. Note the spirit traveling in this orb. This is how they come from the other dimension to our dimension.

Image 10. This image was seen on Christmas Day 2013. It appears that there are spirits visiting the house. You can see numerous faces in this photo.

Now let's discuss apparitions. The word *apparition* is used to describe any kind of visual paranormal manifestation. Remember, the key to this definition is the word *visual*. *Apparition* is taken from the Latin word *apparere* (meaning to appear). In the literal sense, it means to appear, but in the paranormal sense, it covers all visionary appearances, hallucinations, clairvoyance, and other unusual perceptions.

A ghost is a visual apparition of a deceased human being. The term implies that the ghost is a spirit of the person it represents (The Paranormal Dictionary) Chad L. Stambaugh) page 50-51). Throughout history, people have tried to communicate with the spirit world through mediums. This was called *necromancy* until the nineteenth century, when they began calling this conjuring up of spirits a séance.

A full-body apparition is an apparition of a dead person that is the full or almost full figure of a human or other entity that is transparent or solid. I have seen plenty of these apparitions in this house. Some were scary, and others were not.

I saw a woman in a wheelchair in my bedroom after waking up from a nap. It actually looked like my mother-in-law, but she was in a wheelchair. I did see my mother-in-law in a wheelchair while she was in the hospital before she died. So, I think it was her. It appeared for a second and then immediately disappeared. The night before I saw this apparition, my son said he felt someone touch his foot while he was in bed. The apparition did not scare me. I think she was worried about me and my son and was trying to comfort us.

However, in July 2015, there was a scary apparition in my room. My son and I used to go to the cemetery every week to visit my husband's grave and lay down flowers. The last time we went there I saw a scary apparition in my room later that evening. I will tell you what I saw.

I decided to go to bed early that night at around 10:15, as I was tired. I was lying in bed and heard noise near the television set. I thought to myself, *No, there can't be anything here. It's too early.* It turned out that I was wrong. I feel asleep thinking it was just static from the television and woke up seeing a man staring at me from near the corner of the bedroom.

It was near my bed, so when I woke up, I could see it very clearly. It was a black man with afro-textured hair. He looked fairly young, but he was very angry. I started to scream, which usually causes the apparition to disappear right away, but this one did not. My son was still up and heard my screams. He opened my door, and then the apparition disappeared.

This apparition scared the hell out of me because it was so angry. I feel this particular spirit followed us from the cemetery to the house. My son also saw a girl in his room watching him sleep. She peeled his covers down and was looking at him. This also occurred after a visit to the cemetery, so I do not go there anymore. The next day, I developed hives from this scary experience.

We now use an apotropaic sacred object (this object is holy water) to hold these revenants at bay. The word *revenant* is another name for a ghost. The term was used a long time ago and is not really used today except in rare instances. These apparitions of the dead still continue in this house but my son and I are trying to get them under control. This is rather hilarious given the fact that you cannot control the soul, which is actually the name of my first book. *You Can't Control the Soul* is available on Amazon.

When spirits want to come to this dimension, there is absolutely nothing you can do to ward them off. They come here for a purpose. As I said in chapter 1, there are many reasons for their coming. Negative energy and upset will bring them back. When things are fine, they are quiet and do not get upset.

My son and I went out to the store a few days ago in my new car. All of a sudden, while I was driving, we heard four knocks in the back of the car. We knew who this was. My husband will get upset if someone says anything about me or my son. I often wonder if these people who upset us are also being haunted but do not tell anyone about it. Remember, the spirits can appear anywhere and will haunt if provoked.

There are also other types of apparitions. Following is a list with a brief definition of each type.

- Having the characteristics of a human being type of apparition – A distinguishable form that resembles a human.
- Closely-related apparition – A distinguishable member of the family. This is the most common type of apparition we experience.
- Chronicled apparition – From another era, whether it be the past or the future.
- Incognitive apparition – Some concealed or unrecognized form.
- Zoological apparition – An animal, usually a decreased pet. These are very common apparitions, because humans form strong bonds with their pets. Souls of animals can be seen on videos I have taken. We can see cats and dogs in the pictures as well. They are seen with their tongues wagging.
- Idiosyncratic apparition – Nonhuman but with the characteristics of a human.

- Extracelestial apparition – Not of this world; not of this dimension or realm.
- Living apparition – A near-death ghost. It could be a coma patient for example.

Even shadow people are considered apparitions. Shadow people are not evil or demons as most people may think. They are really apparitions of the dead that do not have enough energy to manifest as full-body apparitions. I have seen a few shadow people apparitions in the house. The first was shortly after my husband had died.

I was in my dining room and heard some type of movement in the living room. I got up to see what it was, and as I entered the kitchen to go to the living room, I saw a shadow hiding behind one of the kitchen cabinets. It saw me and immediately disappeared. Another time I was sitting in the living room watching television and happened to see the floor near the television become extremely black. I looked up, and on the stairs I saw a shadow person standing there smiling. It would not look directly at me but looked to the corner of the living room. It then disappeared. It actually looked like my husband, but some of the features were different. The nose looked artificial in shape, and this shadow person cast such a dark shadow on the floor that I was rather afraid.

My son also saw a shadow person sitting in my husband's dining room chair just after his death. I was working at the time, but my son said he heard chopping in the kitchen as though someone was preparing a meal. The cutting board was wet, but there was no food on it. He went downstairs and saw movement in the chair. This shadow was moving back and forth calling my name. It then disappeared. It was quite scary stuff at the time. My son told me about this when I got home, and I told him that what he was claiming was ridiculous. No one could have been there. My attitude changed when I began seeing these hauntings myself.

I feel that the spirits in my house go back and forth to some realm and do not stay here all the time. They could have passed over but come back due to protection and worry for their loved ones.

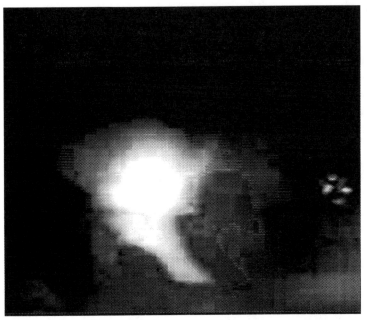

Image 11. Here you can see how the spirits travel from their dimension to ours.

The orb in this image is called a contrail, and the spirits are traveling in this orb. When a spirit is moving about, its shape is an orb with a contrail (also called vapor). When the spirit is at rest, or no longer in motion, the energy of the spirit will expand into an ectovapor or ectoplasm. According to Wikipedia, an ectoplasm (paranormal) is supposed to be a physical substance that manifests as a result of energy.

The word *ectoplasm* was coined in 1894 by Charles Richet to describe a gooey substance that eerily oozed from a psychic medium while in a trance. The word was formed from the Greek words *ektos* and *plasma*. When putting these words together, they mean "outside formed."

Image 12. A medium with ectoplasm coming from her mouth. Of course, this was more of a hoax during the rise of spiritualism and fraudulent mediums.

Today, the term *ectoplasm* has come to represent the physical manifestations of mists believed to be ghosts or spirits. In the movie *Ghostbusters* the green slime emitted by ghosts is described as "ectoplasm residue." The movie talked about being slimed by a ghost, which was its representation of ectoplasm.

Image 13. You can see a mist surrounding this orb. This means the spirit is trying to materialize.

This ectoplasm is a precursor to the formation of an apparition. At times, the mist will be witnessed first, and then the ectoplasmic formation may take on the shape of a human with details such as body features, color, and clothing. This ectoplasm, or mist, can be seen in many paranormal investigations when pictures are taken of hauntings.

A vortex is a very strange phenomena. It looks like a swirling funnel shape when moving about. I have captured a spinning vortex and have put a video on YouTube. (To see the video and watch the phenomena in action, type "spinning vortex spaduzzi 1234" in the YouTube search bar.) This is a unique site to see. You will also see orbs entering the vortex and returning to the spirit world. This video documents the belief that spirits do exist and come back to visit the living in this type of spinning funnel.

There are many spirits that are traveling together in this vortex seen on YouTube. This vortex serves as a vehicle to transport spirits in the shape of orbs from their realm to ours. It is an energy mass that is a temporary opening to the other side. This is the result of spirit energy in motion. This energy creates a sonic boom when it enters the atmosphere. My son and I heard this sound when the vortex appeared in the living room. If only this vortex could be captured and studied, we would learn a tremendous amount of information about the spirit world and their energy.

I wonder how this could be done. What wonders are out there in the spirit world? Where is this world, and what other types of entities occupy it? These are questions that must be investigated and found out. We are only at the beginning of our investigations into the paranormal. I believe this spirit world consists of many different entities, including aliens and possibly demons. We must investigate this and get an answer as to what exists in different dimensions. Only then will we be able to really communicate with the dead and learn from them. They are trying to tell us something in all these hauntings, so please learn.

CHAPTER 3

ALIENS

The most famous documented account of alien abduction was reported by Barney and Betty Hill. This reported abduction took place September 19–20, 1961. The reason this case was taken seriously was because these two people were considered normal, upstanding citizens.

Barney and Betty Hill were an interracial couple. They were driving in their 1957 black and white Chevy Bel Air trying to find suitable lodging that would accept them along with their pet, a dachshund named Delsey. This was going to be their belated honeymoon, as their work commitments forced them to delay their honeymoon. Betty was forty-one years old, and Barney was thirty-nine years old. It was the second marriage for both of them.

The Hills traveled to Vermont, Niagara Falls, and Toronto before heading toward Montreal on September 19. While listening to the radio, they heard a report of approaching tropical storm Esther, so they decided to return home early. They were driving through New Hampshire's White Mountains late that night when they noticed a bright object in the sky. It was flying in an erratic pattern and seemed to be following them. While this was happening, they were on Route 3 traveling through the Franconia Notch mountain pass. They described this craft as being as large as a four-engine plane.

Finally, the Hills returned home at five o'clock in the morning, which was two hours later than they should have arrived. At the time, however, they were unaware of this time difference. Their watches had stopped working, and they finally realized there was a gap of missing time when they saw their clock at home. They wondered why their trip had taken so long.

Barney and Betty Hill had amnesia regarding those missing hours, but when they arrived home, other strange mysteries surfaced. Betty Hill's dress was torn, although she did not recall how or when this had happened. The tops of Barney's shoes were severely scraped, yet he could not remember how it had occurred. They both felt very unclean and took showers, but they did not bathe their dog, which later developed a severe fungal condition.

Betty and Barney Hill's health began to decline, so they decided to go under hypnosis to find out what had happened to them that night. Under hypnosis, Barney described the craft as resembling a big pancake with windows and lights. Its flight was totally silent. Barney had stopped the car and tried to get a better look at the craft using his binoculars. Putting on a leash and walking into a field where the view was better, Barney could see beings in the craft looking back at him. He immediately ran back to the car where Betty was waiting, and they drove away.

All of a sudden, he turned onto a remote side road where five humanoid figures blocked their path. The Hills were surrounded, removed from their car, and taken prisoner by these humanoid figures. Barney resisted capture, and that is how the tops of his shoes became scraped. Once in the aircraft, the couple was separated. While being examined, aliens placed some sort of cup over Barney's groin and left twenty-one lesions that formed a circle.

While under hypnosis, Betty described the aliens as hairless with no earlobes or cartilage, only ear holes. They were aluminum gray in color with big chests and spindly (long and thin) legs. Betty described undergoing medical procedures. The aliens did not pay much attention to the fact that Barney was black and Betty was white, but they were extremely fascinated by the discrepancy in their teeth. Barney had dentures because of injuries during his military service, and Betty's teeth were not removable. Under hypnosis, the Hills were warned never to discuss this experience with anyone, as the aliens would know if the Hills spoke about the abduction and would return to punish them.

In October 1965, the *Boston Traveler* ran a five-day series about the Hills. This newspaper plunged the Hills into the public eye, which they did not want. The Hills finally agreed to speak publicly about their experience for the first time on Sunday, November 7, 1965 at Pierce Memorial Church in Dover, New Hampshire.

The media surrounded the Hills' home and workplaces. Their telephone rank off the hook. Their abduction saga was the subject of John Fuller's 1966 best-selling book *The Interrupted Journey: Two Lost Hours "Aboard a Flying Saucer."* The Hills shared royalties with Fuller. The book did not make them rich, but it made enough money so they could live more comfortably. All three of the passengers on this alien craft—Barney, Betty, and the dog Delsey—deteriorated dramatically. Barney died at the age of forty-six of a cerebral hemorrhage, and Delsey died from a bladder infection and dehydration that did not respond to veterinary care. Betty developed stomach cancer and had 80 percent of her stomach removed. She later developed lung cancer that metastasized to her brain and adrenal glands. She died in 2004.

Image 14. Group of Aliens

Since 1972, sightings and encounters by aliens have been classified into seven types:

- Close encounters of the first kind involve sightings of a UFO.
- Close encounters of the second kind involve discovering evidence of UFOs or extraterrestrials.
- Close encounters of the third kind involve seeing extraterrestrials and/or having contact with them.
- Close encounters of the fourth kind involve alien abductions.
- Close encounters of the fifth kind involve a continuous communication between an alien and a human.
- Close encounters of the sixth kind involve the death of a human being or an animal during an alien encounter.
- Close encounters of the seventh kind involve the genetic interchange between humans and aliens that result in the creation of a hybrid or transgenic being. This particular encounter is discussed later.

Image 15. Picture of the Grey Aliens

Aliens in our midst.

This image is of a gray-skinned humanoid, three to four feet tall, with black almond-shaped eyes, nostrils without a nose, and slits for a mouth. It has small ears and lacks earlobes.

Paul Hellyer was the Canadian Minister of National Defense in the 1960s. He was the highest-ranking person inside the Department of Defense for Canada. The Hon. Paul Hellyer is the highest-ranking person among all countries to openly speak about UFOs and extraterrestrials. He states that there are at least four alien species that have been visiting earth for thousands of years.

I left my recorder one day in the bedroom to see if I could pick up any paranormal sounds or talking by the spirits while I was out. I came home and turned on the recorder, and I heard some type of robotic voice. It did sound like some sort of an alien voice. I couldn't believe what I'd heard. The voice said: "You will have millions." I really did not know what or who made this voice, but I never heard it again.

According to Paul Hellyer, the aliens are very concerned about us using the atomic bomb again. This will affect the entire cosmos, and the aliens are trying to make sure the planet will not be destroyed.

Image 16. Group of Grey Aliens

The grays are associated with alien abductions. This species is thought to be android—biological robots. This is the voice I heard on the recorder. These gray aliens are the ones that maneuver the UFOs (flying saucers) that many people see today.

There is a theory about the Egyptian Pharaoh Akhenaten, who ruled Egypt for seventeen years. He was the Pharaoh of the eighteenth dynasty of Egypt and was the father of Tutankhamun. The theory had to do with this pharaoh who the Egyptians believed came from the stars. In the year 1352 BC, Akhenaten ascended to the throne as the tenth pharaoh of the eighteenth dynasty. When he became Pharaoh, he decided to institute many changes, including religious changes. One such change was a ban on multiple gods. He introduced the worship of the Aten (worshiping the radiant disk of the sun). Upon becoming pharaoh, he ordered all the iconography of previous gods to be removed. He only allowed one emblem—a sun emblem, which was literally a sun disk with strange arms or rays pointing down.

Akhenaten was strange looking, not like other pharaohs. He is depicted with an elongated skull, long neck, sunken eyes, thick thighs, long fingers, backward-turned knee joints, a prominent belly that suggested a pregnancy, and female-like breasts. The strangest feature was the elongated skull. Akhenaten's body was a mixture of feminine and masculine features.

His wife, Nefertiti, was also depicted as having an elongated skull. Was this some type of genetic anomaly that caused their heads to be misshapen and disproportionally large, or as theory suggests, were they a hybrid human being with genes and DNA from extraterrestrials?

Akhenaten was succeeded by his son Tutankhamun, who became the most renowned pharaoh of all time. When his tomb was open by Howard Carter in 1922, Tutankhamun was also found to have an elongated skull. In 2010 the results of DNA tests confirmed that he was the son of Akhenaten.

Image 17. This is a picture of Akhenaten. Note the feminine features.

Image 18. Stone statue in Egyptian Tomb

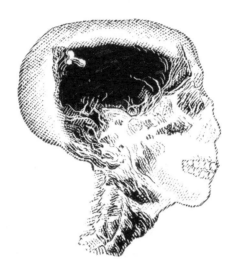

Image 19. Black and white illustration of Tutankhamun's skull.

Image 20. Sculpture of Egyptian queen Nefertiti.

Image 21. This is a picture of Akhenaten's wife, Nefertiti. Note the elongated head.

Image 22. Pharaoh Akhenaten.

Image 22 depicts Pharaoh Akhenaten. The representation of him illustrates a misshapen head, a potbelly, a sunken chest, elongated arms, and larger thighs. These features were opposed to the traditional Egyptian artists who depicted pharaohs as big and strong.

Dr. Irwin M. Braverman, professor of dermatology at Yale University School of Medicine, attributes the king's female form to familial gynecomastia, brought on by an inherited syndrome called aromatase excess syndrome. This diagnosis is the first to be associated with Akhenaten. As for the shape of Akhenaten's head, Dr. Braverman attributes this to a condition called craniosynostosis, in which sutures (the fibrous joints of the head) fuse at an early age and interfere with the process of skull formation. The specific condition is called a sagittal suture, which is dominantly inherited. Dr. Braverman has noted that he observed this abnormality in the king's daughters, as well as in Queen Hatshepsut, daughter of Tuthmosis I, founder of Akhenaten's paternal line, and in King Tut, who ended this line (http://www.ancient-code.com/akhenaten-the heretic-pharaoh/).

But what about his wife, Nefertiti? Why was her skull also so elongated? Was there an influence from aliens? You can decide for yourself!

Now we will talk about another species called the Nordics. They look like regular, good-looking humans with very fair complexions, blonde hair, and blue eyes. My son had a dream about two women with blue eyes and blonde hair injecting him with some type of substance. He told me when he woke up that he felt extremely groggy. I told him about these aliens and what they look like, and he told me his experience while dreaming.

He recalled being in my office sitting down in the chair when two women with blonde hair and blue eyes and dressed in tight-fitting clothes surrounded him. They then gave him some type of injection. When he woke from this dream, he told me, "I could feel the pain of the injection in my arm." Who knows for sure what really happened. I am just relaying what I was told. You can make your own decision.

These Nordics appear quite attractive. Their hair is most always blonde and normally straight and fine. Some have ears, but not all do. Some of these

Nordics have five digits on their hands, and they do resemble humans in many ways. Their eyes are striking and normally blue. They have been described as wearing normal human clothes that enable them to blend in with us while they are here on earth.

Image 23. Nordics.

These aliens look like Northern Europeans (Scandinavians). This particular type of UFO occupant is very interesting because their appearance suggests that the human form is not just native to our own planet, that we may have common ancestors, or they may be time travelers.

Image 24. The reptilian aliens.

These aliens, called the reptilians, have been around since the beginning of mankind and have been thought to have given the human race much of its early technology, helped build the pyramids, worked with the Mayans, and helped start early religions by pretending to be gods and manipulating Adam and Eve in the Bible.

These reptilians, or reptoids, are an alien race made up of human-looking lizard creatures. They are also known as dinosauroids, lizardfolk, lizardmen, Saurians, Alpha Draconians, and Sauroids.

These reptilians are tall, around seven to nine feet; have green, scaly skin; have three long fingers and an opposable thumb with talons (claws) on the ends; have holes for ears and large eyes; and have muscular legs and arms.

They are reported to be a very dangerous alien species bent on the domination of our planet. They are very intelligent, have telekinetic powers, and are known to be evil. One theory suggests that they were native to our planet before the rise of humans and live in secret, underground caverns around the world. Another theory suggests that they come from the Alpha Draconi star system of the Orion constellation. Or both perhaps both theories are true.

The next type of alien being is called the hybrid alien.

Image 25. The hybrid alien.

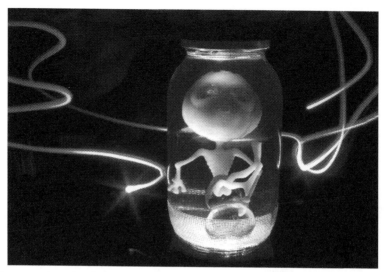

Image 26. Hybrids look human, and some are born into human families.

These hybrid aliens cannot stay in our physical environment for a prolonged period of time. They require psychic or etheric energy to project themselves into our three-dimensional environment. As you can see, spirits and aliens are quite alike in this respect.

The process used in the creation of these hybrid aliens is quite complicated, but following is a brief description.

Both genetic and metaphysical factors must be taken in account, as it is the latter that accounts for the hybrid breeding program taking more time than one might aspect. Human DNA is the interface mechanism between the nonphysical soul and the physical body. For this particular interface to hold both together, genetics must match the soul profile. A slight mismatch in one will cause a mutation in the other, and too much of a mismatch will keep the soul from seating in the body. So to genetically modify or create an entire race, it is not enough to merely engineer the genetic code. That code must be synchronized so its profile and growth match that of the souls intended to occupy the bodies. This is why people with specific bloodlines that resonate with the aliens' own soul nature are targeted for abduction. Their descendants carry some type of imprint that is considered very valuable as stock material for engineering the hybrid race.

Successful hybrids are those who possess the following traits:

- They can survive in our environment indefinitely.
- They can reproduce successfully with both humans and other hybrids.
- They look human enough to integrate easily.
- They are void of any undesirable human traits.

These hybrids are biologically robust like us because they have human bodies, but they will be mentally superior to humans and loyal to the aliens if they have souls identical to them. Alien abductions serve multiple purposes, and this is one of them. Beware of aliens in our midst.

CHAPTER 4

THE AFTERLIFE

The supernatural belief of an afterlife exists. The afterlife is also referred to as life after death, or it can also be called the hereafter. Where is the hereafter? Many people do not understand this concept. They think heaven is up, and hell is down.

In the 1960's, Soviet dictator Nikita Khrushchev laughed at religious people who believed in heaven, because he had sent cosmonauts into space and they had not seen it (From the book:The Soul After Death-Fr. Seraphim Rose).

After physical death, the continued existence of the soul takes place in the spiritual realm. The soul may be reborn into this world and begin the life cycle all over again with no memory of what the soul did in the past. Major views of the afterlife are derived from religions, esotericism (spiritual viewpoints), and the metaphysical. The soul is believed to be immortal.

Reincarnation is the belief that when a person dies, the body decomposes but a part of that person is reborn into another body. The Indian culture believes that a person has lived before and will live again in another body after death. The belief in reincarnation could explain why bad things happen to good people and good things happen to bad people: They are being rewarded or punished for actions in their past lives, which is known as karma.

In the Indian religions, the soul is reincarnated, and this nature of continued existence is determined directly by the actions of the individual in his or her ended life rather than through the decision of another being. This concept of reincarnation is accepted by the Hindu, Buddhists, Jains, Sikhs, Rosicrucians, Theosophists, Spiritists, and Wiccans. This is the concept of karma, where events in our current lives are the consequences of the actions taken in our previous lives.

According the Buddhism, karma differentiates people into low and high states. Our past actions and our current behaviors are responsible for our happiness and misery. We create our own heaven, and we create our own hell. What causes some people to live long lives and some to live short lives, some to be healthy and some to suffer from disease, some to be ugly and some to be beautiful, some to lack any type of influence and some to be powerful, some to be poor and some to be rich, and some to be ignorant and some to be wise? The answer is karma.

The Samyutta Nikaya (The Book of Causation) (From Wikipedia, the free encyclopedia) states: "According to the seed that's sown, So is the fruit that you reap there from, Doer of good will gather good, Doer of evil, evil reaps, Down if the seed and thou shalt taste, the fruit thereof."

This is the belief that the last thought before death will determine the state of a person in his or her subsequent birth. This may be either good or bad karma. Karma teaches individual responsibility and serves as an incentive to do good.

The terms *heaven* and *hell* used in the Abrahamic religions refer to places where the soul goes after death, depending on one's deeds here on earth. Heaven is a place where the righteous go after death and is defined as eternal union with God. Hell is a condition of punishment and torment for the evil, which is eternal separation from God. This is a form of confinement with other sinful souls and the fallen angels.

There is another place we can go to after death called limbo. This particular place was elaborated upon by the theologians beginning in the Middle Ages but was never recognized as dogma of the Roman Catholic Church.

Limbo is the theory that those innocent, unbaptized souls (such as infants) or those who have died before baptism exist in neither heaven nor hell. They are not guilty of any personal sin but still bear original sin. For this reason, these souls are seen existing in a state of natural, but not supernatural, happiness until the end of time. This place was described as an intermediate place of confinement in oblivion and neglect (definition of limbo-Free Online Dictionary, Thesaurus and Encyclopedia."

Now the notion of purgatory is associated particularly with the Catholic Church. This place is for those who die imperfectly purified but are assured of their eternal salvation. After death, they undergo purification in order to achieve the holiness necessary to enter the joy of heaven.

The traditional African religions hold various beliefs. For example, the Hazda have no particular belief in the afterlife; the death of the person is the end of their existence.

In the Ancient Egyptian religion, when the body died, parts of its soul known as *ka* (body double, or your astral body) and the *ba* (personality) would go to the Kingdom of the Dead. The statues in the Egyptian tombs were placed there as substitutes for the deceased (Richard P. Taylor, Death and the afterlife: A Cultural Encyclopedia, ABC-CLIO, 2000).

The Egyptians also believed that being mummified and put in a sarcophagus (an ancient Egyptian coffin) carved with complex symbols, designs, pictures, and hieroglyphs was the only way for the dead to have an afterlife. The Egyptian Book of the Dead was placed in the tomb with the body, along with food, jewelry, and curses.

The Egyptian Book of the Dead was a guide to the afterlife. It outlines what the dead would face in the afterlife. Each mummified corpse was expected to rise in the afterlife, and this book contained spells to aid in the afterlife.

Egyptians also performed a ritual called the opening of the mouth, which was meant to endow statues with the capacity to support the living ka (the body double, or astral body) and receive offerings. This ritual was performed throughout the entire temple structure. This ritual was to reanimate the deceased to eat, breath, see, hear, and enjoy the offerings and provision brought to the temple to sustain the ka.

The priests performing the opening of the mouth ritual would recite this hymn: "Awake! … May you be alert, as a living one, rejuvenated every day, healthy in millions of occasions of god sleep, while the gods protect you, protection being around you every day" (The Opening of the Mouth Ritual by Marie Parsons).

The ancient Greeks believed in an underworld where the spirits of the dead went after death. They believed that unless the proper funeral rites were performed, the deceased person's spirit would never reach the underworld and would then haunt the upper world as a ghost forever.

There was a Greek god called Hades, who was known in Greek mythology as the king of the underworld—a place where souls live after death. The Greek god Hermes, who was a messenger of the gods, would take the soul of the decreased person to the underworld (called either Hades or the House of Hades). The Greek god Hermes would leave the soul on the banks of the River Styx, which was the river between life and death (Social Studies School Service, Ancient Greece, 2003, pp. 49-51.

When the Roman Empire conquered Greece in 146 BC, it took much of Greek religion and incorporated it into its own.

In Judaism, the Talmud offers a number of thoughts relating to the afterlife. After death, the soul is brought for judgment. Those who have lived a pristine life (uncorrupted) will enter immediately into the *Olam Ha-Ba,* or the World to Come. Most souls do not enter the World to Come immediately and experience a period of review (not more than one year) for reschooling and for the soul to gain wisdom as one's errors are reviewed. After this review, the soul will enter the World to Come.

According to Judaism, reincarnation (called *gilgul*) is found in the Yiddish literature among the Ashkenazi Jews. Human souls can end up being reincarnated into nonhuman bodies. There are others who believe in people reincarnating into successive lives, according to Martin Buber's early collection of stories of the Baal Shem Tov's life.

Mainstream Christianity professes belief in the Nicene Creed, which denotes the resurrection of the dead and the life of the world to come. Death is an intermediate state, along with heaven, hell, the Second Coming of Christ, the resurrection of the dead, the rapture, the tribulation, the millennium, the end of the world, the last judgment, a new heaven and a new earth, and the ultimate consummation of all of God's purposes.

Jesus maintained that the time would come when the dead would hear the voice of the Son of God and all those in the tombs who have done good deeds would come out to the resurrection of life, but those who have done wicked deeds would come out to the resurrection of condemnation.

Jehovah's Witnesses believe that after Armageddon there will be a bodily resurrection of the righteous and unrighteous dead. At this time, unrepentant sinners will be punished with eternal death (nonexistence).

The Seventh-day Adventists believe as the Jehovah's Witnesses that God will grant eternal life to the redeemed who are resurrected the Second Coming of Jesus. Until then, all those who have died are asleep.

The Islamic belief in the afterlife stated in the Koran is descriptive. The Islamic word for *paradise* is *Jannah*, and hell is *Jahannam*. Jannah has seven gates and seven levels. The higher the level, the better it is and the happier you are. Jahannam possess seven deep, terrible layers. The lower the layer, the worse it is. All individuals will arrive at everlasting homes on Judgment Day. The Last Day is also called the Day of Standing Up, Day of Separation, Day of Reckoning, Day of Awakening, Day of Judgment, Encompassing Day, or the Hour. God is referred to as Allah.

Until the day of judgment, deceased souls remain in their graves awaiting the resurrection. However, they immediately begin to feel a taste of their destiny to come. Those bound for hell will suffer in their graves, while those bound for heaven will be in peace until that time.

On the Last Day, the resurrected humans and even the jinn will be judged by Allah according to their deeds. The jinn is a class of spirits, lower than the angels, capable of appearing in human and animal forms and influencing humankind for either good or evil. (From the Dictionary. com). The Last Day is depicted as passing over hell on a narrow bridge in order to enter paradise. Those who fall, weighted by their bad deeds, will remain in hell forever.

Unitarian Universalism believes that the soul will ultimately be saved, and there are no torments of hell (Bond, Jon 2004-06-13 Unitarians: Unitarian view of the afterlife, Retrieved 2014-03-08) Most Unitarian Universalists believe that heaven and hell are symbolic places of consciousness, and the faith is largely focused on the worldly life rather than any possible afterlife (Searching for Spiritual Unity-Can There Be Common Ground? Page 582, Robyn E. Lebron-2012.

> I believe in The Other Side and the eternity of the soul. I believe our spirits make the round-trip from this world to The Other Side many times, by our own choice, to learn and experience for the ongoing advancement of the souls God gave each one of us. I believe that only a thin vein separates our earthly dimension from the dimension of The Other Side. I believe that the Other Side is Home, where we all came from and where we will all go again, and that we carry very real memories of it in our spirit minds. And I believe it is on The Other Side, between what we call "lifetimes," that we are really at our most alive. "Life On The Other Side", (Sylvia Browne, New American Library, 2000, Chapter 1).

There definitely is a hereafter (afterlife). I have seen and heard spirits coming here from the spirit world and going back again. Spirits move from one sphere to another. This world of spirits is a place halfway between heaven and hell, and this place is also our halfway state after death. There is a vast number of people in this world of spirits, because that is where everyone is first gathered—where we are all examined and prepared for the next journey. Some people stay for a short period of time in this spirit world, while others stay longer, although no one stays more than thirty years.

God sorts out the evil people and the good people when they arrive in this spirit world. You can see everyone who died in the spirit world, but when you go to either heaven or hell, you do not see them anymore. Because the spirit is alive and not the body, the spirit does the thinking in our bodies. The spirit is the actual person; it's the spirit that keeps us alive and holds our emotions.

Why is it that when I miss my husband at night, my soul goes into astral projection? This is because the soul is seeking relief from emotional distress. It does control the body. The so-called silver cord will guide us to other realms to seek out comfort for our souls. This silver cord is connected to us below the breastbone. It nourishes our spirits with the life force of God's love. This cord keeps us connected to the other side in our brief trips away from home. "Before the silver cord is snapped … and the spirit returns to God who gave it" (Eccles. 12:6–7).

I believe this silver cord is definitely connected below the breastbone. When I woke up the morning after having an astral projection, I could feel a type of pulsation below my heart by my breastbone. It felt like a weakness, and the experience scared me. This happened only one time, and the feeling has not come back ever again.

According to the book *"Afterlife"* by Emanuel Swedenborg, there are three states that we pass through after death before the soul can arrive in heaven or go to hell. "The first state is one of more outward concerns, the second is one of more inward concerns, and the third is one of preparation. We go through these states in the world of spirits" (Afterlife Emanuel Swedenborg page 29).

However, there are some people who immediately go directly to heaven or hell. Those people who go immediately to heaven were regenerated souls and prepared for heaven in this world. Those who were profoundly malicious but disguise it with a guise of goodness will immediately go the hell.

Many religions and many individual people believe in the same concept of the afterlife. We *do* live on. Our spirits continue to learn in the afterlife and continue to help us with our earthly lives.

CHAPTER 5

ORBS

What are orbs? Orbs are supernatural, paranormal phenomena without verifiability, such as invisible spirits, auras, angels, ghosts, energy fields, and energy balls. I have remarkable images of orbs that were captured in my house with my security camera.

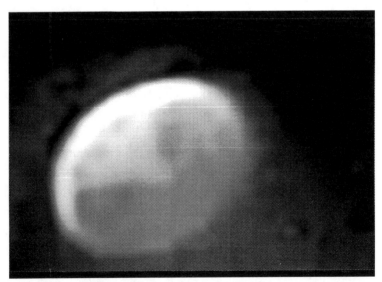

Image 27. You can definitely see another dimension in these orb photographs. This photo looks like a person in the other dimension, along with some type of land in the background. The vibrational rate must be increased to see the other dimension in these orbs. I can only see these orbs in photographs and have never seen one with the naked eye.

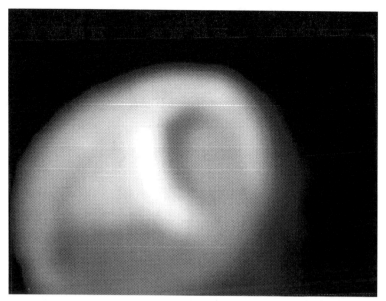

Image 28. Here is an orb with the other dimensions inside.

The spirits travel in these orbs and return the same way. These orbs are here for a purpose and have a job to do. These orbs are low-energy manifestations of either guardian angels, spirit guides, or our loved ones that surround us every day, at all times. Some people can see them with their physical eyes, and some cannot.

God and the Holy Spirit do not show themselves as orbs. It takes a lot of energy for a ghost to manifest itself and do things in the physical world. Orbs are not evil. There are neither demons nor inhuman entities and are usually benign. If you tell them to leave, they will do so. However, they will not go far, because they have a job to do here, usually watching over us or giving us some message. New devices that record paranormal activity enable us to see these orbs in action. There are full-spectrum cameras, a EMF meter (this is a scientific instrument for measuring electromagnetic fields), white-noise generators, digital recorders, ghost boxes, and thermal imaging cameras.

The first type of haunting depicted through orbs is called an intelligent, or human, haunting. These entities have human personalities and human emotions. These particular hauntings are ghosts and spirits that appear in human form. I have seen these apparitions in the form of both men and women in my bedroom many times. They will usually just look at me, but there have been times when one or two of them have spoken.

The very first time I heard one of them speak was when I returned from a cruise and decided to take a nap, as I was very tired from traveling. I went upstairs to my bedroom to lie down, and just as I awoke, there was a man standing right opposite my bed. He looked to be around forty-five years old, and when he spoke, he had an English accent. He held an envelope in his hand and said, "This is for you." He then immediately disappeared. He did not look at me directly but looked to the side of the bed where my husband used to sleep and smiled. I presumed by this that my husband wanted to give me something, maybe some type of letter?

The second type of haunting is called a residual haunting. It is like a piece of film that plays repeatedly with no variation. It will repeat at the same time and place with no awareness of anyone or anything in the current time. It is some type of event that the ghost or spirit will relive over and over again.

Now the third type of haunting is a demonic haunting, or some type of inhuman haunting. This is the most serious and fearful haunting. It is negative and hostile. These hauntings occur in homes where there are psychological issues such as depression, anger, pain, and stress. Such negative entities are attracted to the opening of a doorway into our world. Be careful of Ouija boards, as they may open these doorways to a demonic presence.

There are several techniques used to capture paranormal activity. For electronic voice phenomena, reel-to-reel and cassette tapes can be used to make recordings. Unfortunately, you may have to listen to hours of recordings before hearing a single word or sound. Digital cameras can capture and record paranormal phenomena. New devices are also being created at an amazing rate to capture the paranormal.

Because of all of these new devices to capture and record the paranormal, there are now numerous ghost-hunting groups arising all over the world.

Before they go to these haunted locations, these ghost-hunting groups must protect themselves against these spirits. Otherwise, spirits can attach to the participants at a haunting location, follow them home, and make their lives a living hell.

Now, let's talk about ley lines and how they contribute to the paranormal and the seeing of orbs. These ley lines are alignments and patterns of powerful, invisible earth energy said to connect churches, temples, burial sites, and other location of spiritual or magical importance. They also attract UFOs as navigational aids.

This phrase *ley lines* was coined in the year 1921 by Alfred Watkins, who was an amateur archaeologist (Free encyclopedia Wikipedia). Vortices are formed in the vicinity of these ley lines. Interest in these ley lines began in 1922 with the publication of Watkins's book *Early British Trackways*.

Today, these ley lines have been adopted by new age occultists as sources of power, or energy, which they believe attract aliens in their UFOs. The particular energy ley lines are in certain sites such as Stonehenge; Mt. Everest; Ayers Rock in Australia; Nazca in Peru; the Great Pyramid at Giza; Sedona, ; and Mutiny Bay, among other places. These locations are believed to have special energy (From the Skeptic's Dictionary). These ley lines seem to enhance paranormal activity and UFO experiences here on earth.

CHAPTER 6

ASTRAL PROJECTION

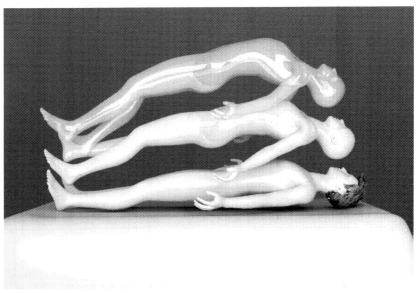

Image 29. Rising of the astral body.

Image 30. The astral body separating from the physical body.

What is astral projection? Astral projection (also called astral travel) is an out-of-body experience achieved while awake, during lucid dreaming, or while in a deep meditation. People who experience astral projection say that their spirits or their astral bodies have left their physical bodies and travel to another dimension known as the spirit world (also called the astral plane).

Psychics say that the subconscious mind (dreaming mind) contains the spirit, or astral body, resulting in dreams containing falling or waking up with a falling sensation or sudden jerk. This sensation reflects the astral body coming back into the physical body. Astral projection also touches on life itself and what happens after physical death.

I remember a time shortly after my husband died. I was in my bed, still awake. It was about two o'clock in the morning, and I was lying down thinking about my husband and how I missed him. I fell asleep, and while sleeping, I felt myself flying in the air down in the living room. I was near the living room window and saw the drapes swaying back and forth from the energy of my astral body.

I could hear my voice calling out my husband's name: "Brad, Brad." My voice sounded different than my regular voice. It was weaker, and I could barely hear it. All of a sudden, I felt my astral body go through the door and downstairs where my son had his bedroom. I saw my husband and other people in the spirit world. He smelled like formaldehyde. Many people are familiar with it in the form of formalin, which is the solution of formaldehyde that is used as an embalming preservative. This is called the smell of death.

I then found myself in a room with a chair, and in the chair, my husband appeared. I looked at his face, and it looked artificial. When he smiled, I could see his mouth and teeth, which looked strange, like a copy of my husband's mouth and teeth. I remember I bent down and gave him a kiss, and then I kissed him again. He smiled at me, and then I don't remember anything else about this particular astral travel.

Another incident happened one night as I was in bed sleeping on my stomach. I woke up in bed and could not move. (This is called sleep paralysis in astral projection.) I felt some type of heavy object pushing into me. I became scared and tried to move and reach for my telephone. I wondered who was pushing into me. It actually felt like an elephant on my back. This entity was strong and persistent about getting into my body. I later figured out it was my soul coming back into my body. Only then, when the pushing stopped on my back, could I move. What an experience this was. It is something I will never forget.

My son has a large mirror in his room, and when he was going through an astral projection, he could see his astral body in the mirror. He told me his astral body looked wispy. It looked fragile and flimsy. It was a weak interpretation of his own physical body he saw in the mirror.

My son says he visits my husband in the spirit world. There are times when my husband tells him, "What are you doing here? It is not your time." There are other spirits with my husband in the spirit world. They also speak to my son and wonder what he is doing there. I told my son please say a prayer to God before you go to sleep and tell him you do not want to have this astral projection. According to the Roman Catholic Church, astral projection is forbidden for Roman Catholics because the soul, which contains all reason, thought, memories, emotion, attitudes, and beliefs, leaves the physical body during the wake state. This can cause bizarre belief systems to develop, based on improperly interpreted sensations from the reality elevated form, and parallel to three-dimensional reality. When we astral project, we are aware consciously of all things that will be encountered when we are out of the physical body.

When the soul is detached from the physical body without the protection of the Roman Catholic God, Jesus Christ, it is very vulnerable to molestation from demons that are encountered in the spirit world during astral projection.

Astral projection refers to the ability to transfer the mind and the consciousness to various astral planes outside the conscious world we live in. The body stays in bed, and the consciousness separates and projects to other astral planes on its own. This astral plane is a spiritual dimension or parallel universe composed of spiritual energy. The term *astral projection* is denoted as an out-of-body experience.

This out-of-body experience happens when a person's soul or spirit leaves the body. Sometimes it travels just a few feet away, while other times it travels as far as to other worlds and dimensions. There are times when the soul needs to be healed from emotional upset here in this dimension and seeks astral projection to get better.

My husband once told me that he was flying around the room and saw me sleeping in the bed. At first, I thought he was only dreaming and told him so. He said to me, "No, no. I saw you sleeping, and I was not sleeping." I now realize this was his soul wanting out of his very sick body. The poor man died two weeks later.

Astral projection helps the soul heal and seek others in the spirit world. My son sees others in the spirit world, but the problem with this is that these spirits will follow him home and haunt him during the night.

Be careful in using astral projection. There are hidden dangers involved in traveling to different planes.

CHAPTER 7

PARANORMAL BEINGS AND THE JINN

Who are the jinn? Do they really exist, or are they some type of fictitious fable?

The jinn are an Islamic belief that is rooted in Arab folklore. There are other cultures in the world that believe in their own type of folklore. In Japan, they are called *oni*; in China, they are the *shen*; in India, they believe in *asuras*; and in Ireland and Scotland, they are called the *fae*.

Is there really a world parallel to our own? The true explanation of the jinn is explained through Islam. It is through the realm of the unseen that Islam explains the world of the jinn.

The jinn were created from fire, angels were created from air, and humans were created from the earth. According to Islam, Allah created the jinn to worship Allah. Like humans, they will also be subject to the final reckoning by Allah. They will be present with mankind on the Day of Judgment and will either go to paradise or hell. The jinn can possess people. A good example of this is depicted in the movie *The Exorcist*. The world of the jinn is sinister and intriguing.

I feel that the jinn are nothing but demons that try to destroy the world through evil and deception. The word *demon* is taken from the Greek word *daimon* (*daimonion*), which was described by the Greek as any type of evil activity in nature. The Greek described the jinn as being demons.

Today, the term *demon* refers to any type of supernatural entity that has an evil intent. This description of a demon would include evil spirits, fallen angels, false gods, unclean spirits, and even the jinn. I feel that there could be some type of evil spirits coming to my house to haunt me and my son. You can see some type of evil activity in images 1 and 2 in this book. What type of spirit is coming out of those orbs? This is a real concern for me and my son. I feel that the portal is left open, and these evil entities come through it to haunt me and my son.

You can call them jinn or something else, but they are nothing but evil spirits and must be cast out by a priest. This can be done through an exorcism. God can bring about the end of any of his creation. We can cast out demons (jinn) in the name of Jesus.

In addition to demons and jinn, there are other paranormal beings that occupy the afterlife. These paranormal beings are seen in near-death experiences. When we die, we can travel with our loved ones who have died to the other realm. We will be embraced by a powerful and profound love and light. We will see our deceased love ones waiting to meet us when we are ready to cross. We will rise up out of our bodies when we die in a mist (astral body), or a globe of light. When we get to the other realm, we will have our life review. There are different levels in the afterlife, and these levels depend on what type of spiritual life we have lived here on earth.

> *To the well-organized mind, death is but the next great*
> *adventure.*

> —J.K. Rowling, *Harry Potter and the Sorcerer's Stone*

Paranormal phenomena are made up of a vast list of entities, including ghosts, demons, hauntings, UFOs, cryptozoology, myths, legends, and metaphysical phenomena. These paranormal beings can take part in after-death communication, which is the most common type of psychic, paranormal experience reported. This happens when someone sees an apparition of a loved one after death. This may occur weeks, months, years, or even decades after passing. Smells associated with a loved one—perfume or cigar smoke, for example—can appear out of nowhere. This is absolutely true, as my son and I can smell my husband's colostomy bag from time to time.

My husband was in intensive care with respiratory failure. While on the respirator, he suffered from a perforated colon. The doctors had to operate and perform a colostomy. When he was home, he used the bathroom downstairs, and we could smell the disgusting odor of his colostomy bag. I sometimes wonder why he wanted us to remember that smell. Well, when we smelled that odor after his death, we knew he was here in the house. I opened the door to the family room one night and saw a white light just standing near the bathroom where my husband used to go to change his colostomy bag. The spirit was probably confused, because I'd had the bathroom turned into a closet. It looked like the spirit was trying to return to a familiar area in the house.

In late 2015, my son and I began experiencing knocking noises in the van. One particular day, I was driving, and all of a sudden we heard four knocks coming from the back of the van. We also noticed something that smelled like lilies and a touch of formaldehyde. This smell comes and goes on occasion.

At the moment of death, often in the final moments, the dying see the dead. Loved ones who have crossed over come back to visit. I remember seeing my father in the intensive care unit as soon as he died. I knew he was extremely cold, because I kissed his face, but the expression on his face was that of extreme ecstasy and euphoria. Who knows what or whom he saw at the moment of death, but I will never forget his face. I do know these deathbed visions, which were once considered just hallucinations, are now part of the dying process. I believe they confirm the fact that there is no death and that there are no dead.

When my mother died, I left the house and went to Connecticut to stay with my fiancé. I was sleeping in the bedroom, and my fiancé was in his office. I woke up in the bed and saw two shafts of light near the door. They started to move toward me, and I became so scared that I closed my eyes. When I opened my eyes, they disappeared. I think they were my mother and father watching over me to make sure I was all right. My father died January 13, 1978, and my mother died May 6, 1978, just four months later. She could not live without my father and had a heart attack in her sleep and died.

Let's discuss these paranormal entities in detail.

What is a demon, and would we ever come across one in our lifetime?

The topic of demonology is a very popular paranormal topic nowadays. The famous demonologists Lorraine and Ed Warren have written numerous books on the subject of demons. Ed Warren was a demonologist, and his wife, Lorraine, is a trance medium. It is their belief that both the devil and God exist. They have written many books and have helped a tremendous number of people conquer evil. The Warrens claimed to have investigated ten thousand cases during their career.

Ed Warren also wrote a book titled *Werewolf: A True Story of Demonic Possession* (St. Martin Press, 1991) ISBN 0-312-06493-4. is a true story of a man named William Ramsey who the Warrens believed was possessed by a demon. The Warrens arranged for an exorcism to be performed on this man, which resulted in a supernatural battle between good and evil.

> Even a man who is pure in heart
> And says his prayers by night
> May become a wolf when the wolfsbane blooms
> And the autumn moon is bright.
>
> Written by Curt Siodmak, a novelist and screenwriter, for his
> 1941 screenplay of The Wolf Man.

Of course, good won over evil, but the battle continues to this day.

I remember one night I came home from work, and my son was very upset because he was being haunted when I went to work. I was upset by this situation and went into each room of the house screaming, "Get out! Get out of my house!" I did this over and over again. Later that night I heard growling in my bedroom near the door. I looked up and saw a crazy-looking thing on the ceiling. It looked like a jack-in-the-box, but what came out was horrible. It looked like a crazy man with jagged teeth. I just looked at this thing without becoming scared, and it then disappeared. I can't be sure what the thing was, but I think it was some form of an evil entity. I feel that there is good and evil in our house because of the portal. I have to be careful not to agitate these things, because they are capable of a lot.

Now let's discuss the other types of paranormal beings that are listed in the supernatural and paranormal encyclopedia. I have included just a sample of these paranormal beings: (Taken from the Wikipedia, the free encyclopedia the Supernatural and the Paranormal).

- Antichrist. One who denies or opposes Christ; *specifically*: a great antagonist expected to fill the world with wickedness but to be conquered forever by Christ at his second coming" (Merriam-Webster, s.v. "Antichrist").

- Angels (guardian angels). This is an angel assigned to protect and guide a particular person, group, kingdom, or country. The belief in guardian angels can be traced throughout all antiquity. A guardian angel pulled me up from the water when I was drowning as a little girl.

- Bigfoot (Sasquatch). "The name given to a cryptid simian ape- or hominid creature that is said to inhabit forests, mainly in the Pacific Northwest region of North America" (Wikipedia, s.v. "Bigfoot").

- Bogeyman. One of those paranormal entities created by the human mind.

- Christmas spirit. This is a subconscious-like entity of harmonious good will. This fuels people to give gifts and donate time to charity, which will refuel the spirit.

- Chupacabra. This creature has elements of reptile, vampire, and demon DNA in its blood. Do not engage this animal or run from it. Please walk away slowly and never make eye contact with it.

- Devil. This is "a supernatural entity that is the personification of evil" (Wikipedia, s.v. "devil"). It is the archenemy of God.

- Demi-zombies. The first known zombie was created in 4129 BC. These are undead creatures, which are usually depicted as mindless, reanimated human corpses with a hunger for human flesh. These zombies are most commonly found in horror and fantasy genre works. *Night of the Living Dead*, for example, is a movie that depicts these so-called zombies in action. Zombies are the walking dead. They are corpses that have typically been reanimated through black magic and in one case by death himself.

- The extraterrestrial aliens and UFO's. These beings were first reported in ancient history, as well as during the past sixty years. Humans were not the first intelligent beings to evolve on earth, but rather the second. The first were reptilelike humanoids that evolved from dinosaurs approximately 65 million years ago (See images 15, 16, and 24). These aliens are called the grays and are discussed earlier in this book.

- Fairies. These are incredibly powerful beings that come in various shapes and sizes and originate from a realm separate from ours.

- Ghouls. These are scavenger creatures that live in graveyards and traditionally feed on the flesh and blood of the dead. At times, ghouls will change their diet and will feed on living humans instead of the dead.

- Guide, or spirit. A spirit that will assist an individual in that person's spiritual journey.

- Hobgoblin. This is a mischievous spirit that delights in perpetrating pranks upon hapless humans. Hobgoblins were dreaded throughout Europe and the Celtic region.

- Inhuman spirit. A spirit that was never human—for example, a demon.

- Jumbie. The ghost or spirit of a person dead who was evil during his or her life will become a jumbie (Montserrat Folklore).

- Kere. Spirit of the dead in ancient Greece. In mythology, the keres are akin to the goddess of death who originally escaped from Pandora's box.

- Legion. Term used to describe a multitude of evil spirits.

- Malicious spirits. A spirit that is evil or spiteful. These spirits destroy or damage things of personal or financial value for the sake of hurting others.

- Night wanderers. An ancient Greek term to denote ghosts.

- Onryo. A Japanese term meaning "angry ghosts or spirits." These ghosts are commonly female and are vengeful spirits that were murdered, abused, or betrayed by their husbands. They usually torment their living husbands in retribution.

- Poltergeist. German for "noisy spirits." Poltergeist can imitate foul odors and make strange rapping, popping, or scratching noises. Apparitions are rare in poltergeist cases.

- Revenant. Another name for a ghost. The term was used long ago and is rarely used today.

- RI. An aquatic creature in Japanese mythology described as a mix between a human and a jellyfish.

- Sanguinon. A person exhibiting vampiric tendencies and powers.

- Tash. Irish name for a ghost that can appear in either human or animal form.

- Vampire. A mythical creature that rises up out of its grave at night to feed on the blood of others.

- Wizard. A male sorcerer and conjurer who is very adept and experienced at his craft.

- Xing-Xing. A possible undiscovered species of orangutan thought to live in southern China.

- Yurei. A Japanese term that literally means "hazy or faint spirit" but is often interpreted in English as a ghost.

- Zlokobinca. A Slavic name for witch meaning "evil dealer."

CHAPTER 8

PORTALS AND VORTICES

I discussed portals and vortices in small detail earlier in the book, but I would like to elaborate on these two very important supernatural and paranormal conditions.

First, what is a portal? Portals are openings between the physical world and the other side—doors to the other dimension. Researchers believe that there are places all over the world that serve as doorways from one world to another.

These doorways are thought to provide access for entities to enter our world. These entities may be spirits of the dead and even otherworldly beings from another dimension. In images 2 and 3 you can see the results of these portals. Numerous spirits arrive from this opening, and these spirits were in the living room as indicated on my security camera. These pictures really looks like some type of horror movie playing out in my living room.

Portals are like swinging doors that spirits can enter or leave through. There are at least three types of portals. The first type of portal is strictly an exit portal and allow those who have died or are close to death to cross into the afterlife. These exit portals are not fixed to one location and can move from time to time.

The second type of portal is called an entrance portal and enable souls to enter into the physical world at birth or in times of great need. These portal doors swing both ways and are harder to locate. A wall could be a portal. In my bedroom, one of the walls near my bed makes noise from time to time. When I use the EMF sensor, there are times it will go off like crazy. This sensor measures the fluctuation in electromagnetic fields. I feel that when I sleep, this is the location where the spirits will come out and where the paranormal activity comes from.

Another type of portal is located at Stonehenge and the Great Pyramid at Giza. These portal doors swing both ways, and there seems to be a lot of soul traffic around these portals. Ley lines have a lot to do with these portals. The Great Pyramid at Giza and Stonehenge are positioned at points where several ley lines intersect each other and then continue on. The spot where these ley lines meet is a source of great power. You can actually feel this tremendous energy and power running through the earth at these points.

Cemeteries are known doorways for the spirit world. The Native Americans chose their burial grounds according to their belief that these burial grounds were scared, spiritual places and believe that these cemeteries were already doorways to the spirit world before they were used as cemeteries.

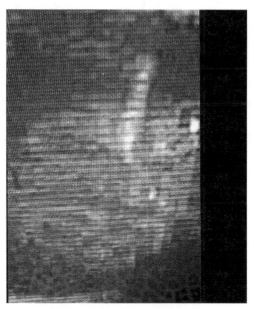

Image 31. Picture of a portal outside the house. You can see different types of entities in this picture.

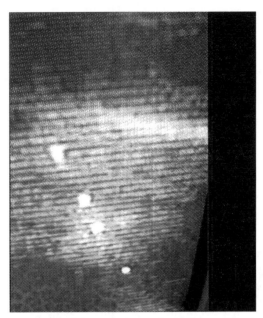

Image 32. Again, a picture of the portal outside the house. You can see numerous entities in this picture.

Image 33. Another portal in front of the house with an orb. You can see faces of the entities in this photo. As I look at this picture carefully, I can also see a beast in this picture.

In the book *Merging Dimensions: The Opening Portals of Sedona* by Tom Dongo and Linda Bradshaw, you can see the same type of portal pictures. These portals outside my house may have moved to different locations as these pictures were taken, because they appeared on the security camera at different times. The portal outside the house near the hedges, for example, may be a portal that has moved to different locations from time to time.

Merging Dimensions contains some good photos of entities in these portals. On page seventy, there is a picture of some type of humanoid figure in the photo. The photo really resembles the camera images I have captured in and around my house, which makes me come to the conclusion that my house either has many portals or one portal that moves around. After reading this book on portals around Sedona, Arizona, I realized there is definitely quite a lot of paranormal activity around the area, as well as many portals. Sedona is said to have four energy vortexes. This is a very interesting book, and the authors have captured some good photos of paranormal activity.

There are many well-known portals or unexplained phenomena in geographic areas around the United States. A few of the supposed portals around the country include the Bridgewater Triangle in Massachusetts, Skinwalker Ranch in Utah, the Bennington Triangle in Vermont, and San Luis Valley in Colorado. These portals are known gateways to weird, unexplainable events and creatures.

Bigfoot is one of those creatures seen in these areas. As you know, the purpose of a portal is believed to be an entry/exit site from this world to another, either another dimension or a parallel universe.

There have been reports of diverse paranormal activity at the portal located in the Bridgewater Triangle. This area is located just thirty miles south of Boston and encompasses a two hundred square-mile triangular area with the towns of Abington, Freetown, and Rehoboth at its corners. The town of Bridgewater is located nearly dead center within the triangle. The area also includes six other towns: Raynham, Taunton, Brockton, Mansfield, Norton, and Easton.

The Hockomock Swamp, which is a five thousand-acre area, lies within the western section of Bridgewater Triangle. This is the hub of many paranormal reports and an eight thousand-year-old Native American burial ground. Paranormal activity was first reported way back in 1760. Since then, this area has spawned many diverse reports that include paranormal events such as ghost dancers, UFOs, and cryptozoological sightings of Bigfoot.

The paranormal area in the Bridgewater Triangle includes low-lying UFOs, sightings of bigfoot, sightings of thunderbird (giant birds with a wing span as great as twelve feet), a large phantom dog with red eyes seen killing two ponies, cattle mutilations, and strange creatures, including giant turtles, black panthers, and snakes as thick as tree trunks. Indian curses are also believed to be active in the area. Of course, hauntings have been reported here, and spook lights have been seen on a number of occasions.

The Bennington Triangle, located in southwestern Vermont, is another area where a portal is reported. There have been a number of people who have gone missing in this area. Many strange happenings have been reported in Glastenbury and the surrounding area for many years prior to the disappearances in the 1940s. The best-known of these cases is probably the disappearance of Paula Jean Welden, which was reported in 1946. Other reported disappearances include Middie Rivers (1945), James Tedford (1949), Paul Jepson (1950), and Frieda Langer (1950). Between 1945 and 1950, these five people disappeared in the Bennington area.

Middle Rivers was seventy-four years old when he disappeared while out hunting. Rivers was guiding a group of four other hunters up the mountains. Going back, Rivers got ahead of the group and was never seen again. There was an extensive search to find Rivers, but he was never seen again. This disappearance occurred in the Long Trail Road area along Vermont Route 9. Rivers was a very experienced hunter and fisherman and was familiar with the local area. (Taken from Wikipedia, the free encyclopedia, Bennington Triangle).

Paula Welden, age eighteen, disappeared about one year later on December 1, 1946. Paula was a sophomore at Bennington College. She was out for a hike on the Long Trail. She was seen on the trail by an elderly couple who said that she turned a corner in the trail, and when they reached the same corner, she had disappeared. When she never returned to college, there was an extensive search for her with a posting of a five thousand-dollar reward and help from the FBI (Frye 2007). No evidence of her was ever found.

Another disappearance took place when a veteran named James E. Tedford disappeared on December 1, 1949. This was exactly three years after Paula Welden's disappearance. Tedford was a resident of the Bennington Soldiers' Home. He went to St. Albans to visit relatives and returned on the local bus but then vanished. A witness claimed that Tedford got on the bus and was still on the bus at the last stop before arriving in Bennington. Somewhere between the last stop and Bennington, Tedford disappeared. His belongings were still in the luggage rack, and an open bus timetable was on his vacant seat (Frye, Todd (2007) "The Bennington Triangle Weird-encyclopedia.com").

The fourth person to disappear was eight-year-old Paul Jepson. On October 12, 1950, Jepson had accompanied his mother in a truck. She got out to feed some pigs and left her son unattended. His mother was gone for about one hour, and when she returned, her son was gone. There were search parties formed to look for the boy, but nothing was ever found. Bloodhounds tracked the boy to a local highway, where, according to local legend, Paula Welden had disappeared four years earlier.

The fifth disappearance occurred sixteen days after Jepson had vanished. Fifty-three-year-old Frieda Langer was out on a hike with her cousin Herbert Elsner when she slipped and fell into a stream. She told Elsner that if he would wait there, she would go back to the campsite, change clothes, and catch up with him. When she did not return, Elsner made his way back to the campsite. He discovered Langer had not returned, and nobody had seen her since they had left. During the next two weeks, five searches were conducted involving aircraft, helicopters, and up to three hundred searchers. No trace of the woman was found. On May 12, 1951, her body was found near the Somerset Reservoir in an area that had already been extensively searched seven months earlier. Because of the long time the body had been exposed to the elements, no cause of death could be determined.

Langer was the last person to disappear and the only one whose body was found. There had not been any direct connection identified that ties these cases together other than the general geographic area and the time period (Frye 2007).

There were reports of weird sounds, noises, and even odors that would come from the mountain. All of these accounts, plus the disappearances of these five people, document the existence of paranormal happenings. There were even sighting of Bigfoot in the mountain area. There was a pattern to the disappearances of the above people. These victims ranged from age eight to seventy-four and were evenly divided between men and women. Time is also a pattern here. The disappearances all happened during the last three months of the year, and many of them were last seen between three and four o'clock in the afternoon.

Of course, alien abduction should also be considered. There have been many reports of UFO sightings and strange lights in the sky that have been spotted over the Glastenbury wilderness during the past century. An American journalist named John A. Keel used the term *window areas* to describe these places, which he believed to be some sort of interdimensional doorway or vortex into another world. There are still strange occurrences happening in this area today (The Vanished Town of Glastenbury and the Bennington Triangle by Chad Abramovich) posted April 7, 2015.

Skinwalker Ranch is the next mysterious place to discuss here.

There have been UFO sightings here, poltergeist-like activity, interdimensional portals, humanoid sightings, and even mutant wolf-like encounters.

Skinwalker Ranch is located in the eerie Uintah Basin of northwestern Utah surrounded on three sides by mountains and cliffs. People believe this area is an interdimensional doorway to another realm.

In 1994 Terry and Gwen Sherman purchased a 480-acre ranch in the basin area. Strange occurrences started happening as soon as they moved in. One really strange and scary occurrence involved a gigantic wolf. A large wolf approached them as they stood outside with Terry's father, Ed. This wolf was larger than any wolf they have ever seen. Both Terry and his father were more than six feet tall, and the wolf was easily chest height on both of them.

At first, the wolf acted like a lost pet, eager for attention. Terry had unloaded several prized Angus calves into a nearby pen. After a few moments, the wolf darted over to the pen and grabbed a calf by the head and attempted to pull it through the bars of the corral.

Terry and his father attempted to save the calf by kicking the wolf in the ribs and then beating it with a stick of wood, but the wolf wasn't deterred.

Terry yelled for his son to get his gun. As soon as Terry had the gun, he shot the wolf twice at point-blank range. Both bullets hit their mark, which should have killed the enormous beast, but it was unfazed by the assault. It continued to pull the distressed calf from the pen, showing no signs of injury. Terry shot the wolf a third time, which finally seemed to get the wolf's attention. It then released its hold on the calf, backed off a few feet, but still didn't run away. Terry shot the wolf a fourth time, striking it in the heart, which should have been a fatal blow, but the wolf still wasn't harmed.

Terry's father retrieved a shotgun from this truck and shot the wolf again. This time the results were visible. A flurry of fur and flesh flow into the air. The wolf backed off several more feet and was looking at them with an icy stare.

Ed took another shot and hit the wolf in the chest. The wolf then started to walk away, and when they attempted to pursue it, they were mystified to discover that the tracks suddenly ended. It was as though the wolf had vanished into thin air.

The family then began noticing other odd occurrences, such as strange balls of light that seemed to hover in the sky. They were noticing orbs and hearing voices that seemed to come from directly over their heads. They started seeing faces in the windows, which turned into apparitions standing at the foot of their beds. This has been happening in my house for the last ten years.

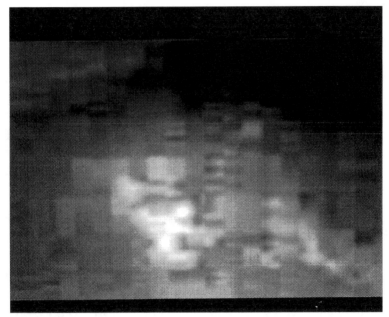

Image 34. Face in window.

There were now cattle mutilations at the ranch. Some cattle had their genital areas mutilated, while another had its eye completely removed, as if done surgically. Next, the cattle began disappearing at an alarming rate, leaving a trail of hoof imprints behind them.

After reading all the strange occurrences at this ranch, you can only reach the conclusion that there is a portal there with UFO activity.

The next portal is located in the San Luis Valley of Colorado. In this area, there have been numerous reports of UFOs, ghosts, crypto creatures, cattle mutilations, Indian legends, portal areas, and even covert military activity.

The Silver Cliff Cemetery in the San Luis Valley was established in the early 1880s and is known for mysterious lights that float around at night. Some say they are the spirits of lost miners who still wander the earth (Wikipedia).

This area is another paranormal playground.

CHAPTER 9

THE BERMUDA TRIANGLE

The Bermuda Triangle is a real supernatural condition. It is one of the most heavily traveled areas in the world, with numerous ships crossing through it on a daily basis from ports all over the world. Cruise ships are also very plentiful in this area. When I have taken cruises to Bermuda, I have heard the ship's captain announce: "We are now right in the middle of the Bermuda Triangle." It's as if he were warning the passengers to brace themselves in case something were to happen.

The earliest reports of unusual disappearances in the Bermuda area appeared in September 17, 1950, article published in the Miami Herald (Associated Press "E.V.W. Jones AP article"(http://www.physics.smu.edu/pseudo/BermudaTriangle/evwjones.html) Retrieved 1 October 2014. The Bermuda Triangle also known as the Devil's Triangle, but according to the US Navy, the triangle does not exist, and the name is not recognized by the US Board on Geographic Names. USCG: Frequently Asked Questions" http://www.history.navy.mil/faqs/faq8-1htm), Uscg.mil.2008-07-22. Retrieved 20 November 2012.

The strange disappearances in this area have also been attributed to extraterrestrial beings. The idea of these extraterrestrial beings being responsible for the strange occurrences and disappearances was used by Steven Spielberg for his science fiction movie *Close Encounters of the Third*

Kind, which features the lost Flight 19 aircraft aircrew members as alien abductees.

Some believe there are natural explanations for all of these rare occurrences. Following are just a few of these theories:

- Compass variations. This is one of the most cited phrases in many of the occurrences along the Bermuda Triangle.
- Gulf Stream. This Gulf Stream is a major surface current. It is primarily driven by thermohaline circulation that originates in the Gulf of Mexico and flows through the Straits of Florida into the North Atlantic. In essence, it is a river within an ocean, and like a river, it can and does carry floating objects. It has a surface velocity of up to about two and a half meters per second (Phillips, Pamela "The Gulf Stream" (http:/fermi.jhuapl.edu/student/phillips/). USNA/John Hopkins. Retrieved 2007-08-02. If a small plane or boat were making a landing because of engine trouble, the current could easily carry it away because of the Gulf Stream.
- Human error. This is the most cited error when it comes to the loss of aircraft or other vessel.
- Violent weather. Tropical cyclones, which form in tropical waters, are very powerful storms that have taken thousands of lives and caused billions of dollars in damage.

Let's talk about the famous Flight 19. This flight was a training flight of five TBM Avenger torpedo bombers that disappeared on December 5, 1945, while over the Atlantic. The squadron's flight plan was scheduled to take them due east from Fort Lauderdale for 141 miles, north for 73 miles, and then back over a final 140-mile leg to complete the exercise. The flight never returned to base. The Navy investigated and came to the conclusion that there was a navigational error that led to the aircraft running out of fuel. A PBM Mariner was deployed with a thirteen-man crew to search and rescue Flight 19, and in the process, the Mariner with all those men on it also disappeared.

The *Carroll A. Deering* was a five-masted schooner that was built in 1919. It was the victim of piracy and possibly involved another ship, the SS *Hewitt*, which disappeared at roughly the same time. There was speculation that the *Hewitt* was involved in the *Deering* crew's disappearance.

Star Tiger and Star Ariel were two flights that disappeared over the Bermuda Triangle. The Star Tiger disappeared on January 30, 1948, during a flight from the Azores to Bermuda, and the Star Ariel disappeared on January 17, 1949, during a flight from Bermuda to Kingston, Jamaica. They were both British South American Airways planes.

A Douglas DC-3 disappeared on December 28, 1948, during a flight from San Juan, Puerto Rico, to Miami. The aircraft and the thirty-two people onboard were never found.

Connemara IV was a pleasure yacht that was found adrift in the Atlantic south of Bermuda on September 26, 1955.

All of the above incidents were the result of some type of paranormal occurrence, in my opinion. As indicated in this book, the paranormal and supernatural can be a very dangerous, unexplained phenomenon. Just like my house with its unexplained orbs, apparitions, shadow people, noises, missing and reappearing objects, knocking on walls, vortex in the living room, and moving portal, the paranormal can also have its effect on planes and ships in the vicinity of the Bermuda Triangle. I believe there is a portal that opens up to a vortex that pulls these ships and aircraft into it. While in the vortex, the missing planes and aircraft, along with the crew, will arrive in another dimension and are not of this plane of existence anymore. I believe that these ships and aircraft were caught up in some sort of time warp and never seen again.

According to the book *Bermuda Triangle True Stories: Paranormal Mysteries (The Little Book of Famous World Mysteries) 2015-8* by Graham Willmott, "To this day, the American military has a standing order to keep a watch for Flight 19, as if they believed it had been caught up in some bizarre time warp and might return at any time." In this book, Willmott indicates that he agreed with the insurance company Lloyds of London that all of these occurrence in the Bermuda Triangle are no mystery and have natural, plausible explanations. The Coast Guard has known the reason for the loss of a craft in almost every case if people would only ask them. I do not agree with this conclusion.

There are many good books and opinions on the Bermuda Triangle that you can read to make your own decisions on this particular phenomenon. Is the Bermuda Triangle a gigantic vortex with opening portals, or is this just a myth? You must decide for yourself.

CHAPTER 10

DEATH AND THE SOUL

When we die, is it the beginning, or is it the end of ourselves? I know that we fear death. We regret leaving our loved ones, and we fight and kick to stay in this world. I believe we are afraid to be judged by God when we die. Most of us learn from our mistakes, and we will return home to the other plane of existence and be judged for the things we did or did not do in our lifetimes.

We decide how we want to leave this mortal existence. We think about the type of death we have not experienced yet in any of our lifetimes. Some decide to leave this earth through a car accident, an airplane crash, a fire, a heart attack, or by just not waking up.

Now, when does the soul really enter the physical body? Many people believe it happens at the time of conception. It may choose to experience life in the womb (around the fourth month) as I indicated earlier, or the soul may want to wait until birth. According to Luke 1:41, "And it came to pass, that, when Elisabeth heard the salutation of Mary, the babe leaped in her womb." This is an example of the soul slipping into the physical body while in the womb.

People in comas have their souls slipping in and out of their physical bodies. That's why comatose patients have out-of-body experiences. Every physical body has a scheduled departure time, and there is no changing it. When my husband died, I was not there. I spoke to a very well-known psychic who told me that each person has an appointed time. I could not have changed anything even though I was not there. In fact, she told me my husband did not want me or my son there when he died. Only God knows the exact time the individual soul will depart from the physical body.

My astral body was in my bedroom one night, and I saw two people standing over my bed. They asked me to come with them, and I asked them, "Who determines death?"

They said, "God. God does."

Of course, I did not go with them, as I have a son to take care of who is disabled.

Before my mother died, she told me she did not want to grow really old. I found her dead in her bed at the age of sixty-five. She had died of an apparent heart attack.

The soul is older than time and has lived many physical lives. Your soul remembers past memories of its other lives. The soul survives death even though the body is dead. "Then shall the dust return to the earth as it was: and the spirit shall return unto God Who gave it" (Ecclesiastes 12:7)." All go unto one place; for all are of the dust, and all turn to dust again" (Ecclesiastes 3:20). The soul does not sleep, but the body does. We all know the body is *not* the whole man. Man is considered the trinity—body, soul, and spirit.

We can say that the dead are alive! According to the above statements, only the body dies, and the soul (or spirit) continues to exist in a conscious state. Also, according to this statement, "For the living know they will die; but the dead do not know anything, nor they any longer a reward, for their memory is forgotten" (Eccles. 9:5). This means the dead body does not exist anymore, but the soul continues to exist.

According to the book *Journey of Souls* by Michael Newton, there is immortality of the soul. He mentions in his book that the soul leaves heaven through a tunnel in order to enter the body of an infant. Souls can arrive in the infant's body any time before, during, or slightly after the moment of birth. This is a very good book to read if you want to know about what happens to the soul at the time of death.

Now to repeat what I have discussed earlier, the soul continues to exist, but the earthly body's state after death is inanimate. According to the writings of Emanuel Swedenborg, after death, we immediately come into the presence of the Lord. This presence fills us with a greater sense of peace, as well as a greater clarity about the troubled areas of our lives. Swedenborg also notes that the process of death is described figuratively in the book of Revelation.

In the first three chapters of Revelation, the Lord appears in person to John and then says, in effect, to the seven churches, "You've done some good things; you've done some things that weren't so great; I invite you to repent." Next, the seven seals are opened, then seven trumpets sound, and then seven bowls are poured out. These can be seen as the various phases of evaluation and treatment we go through when we are in the Lord's presence.

Plato developed the idea of the immortality of the soul in *Phaedo*. According to Plato, a person is an immaterial soul temporarily imprisoned by a body. Death is liberation from the prison of the body, but after an interval of disembodied existence, the soul is again imprisoned and is born again into this world. In Plato's view, all this occurs in the natural course of things (Death and the Afterlife by Lynne Rudder Baker introduction).

Now, according to Christian doctrine, the belief in the immortality of the soul was connected to the belief in the resurrection of the body. Christians believed that Jesus rose from the dead, and his soul survived death of the body and was "reinvested with his risen body" (Wolfson 1956–57, 8). The surviving souls, at the end of time, would be "reinvested" with risen bodies. During the interval between death and the general resurrection, a soul would have a life without a body, but the person's final state would be embodied in some sense. So, when you believe in the Christian doctrine, believe in the resurrection, which includes an immortal soul and post-mortem bodies (Death and the Afterlife by Lynne Rudder Baker, 467).

Many believe that when people die, their souls/spirits are sent to a "temporary" heaven or hell where they await the final resurrection (the final judgment). This will determine the finality of each soul's eternal destination. If you believe that you will go to heaven or hell immediately at death, then why would there be a resurrection?

"At the resurrection of believers, the physical body is resurrected, glorified, and then reunited with the soul/spirit. The reunited and glorified body-soul-spirit will be the possession of believers for eternity in the new heavens and new earth". (Rev. 21–22). "Unbelievers will ultimately be sent to the lake of fire" (Rev. 20:11–15). "These are the final, eternal destinations of all people, based entirely on whether they had trusted Jesus Christ alone for salvation" (Matt. 25:46; John 3:36).

I think the poem entitled "Do Not Stand At My Grave and Weep" written in 1932 by Mary Elizabeth Frye will sum up what I feel about the above information given to you and my idea of death and the soul.

> Do not stand at my grave and weep
> I am not there. I do not sleep.
> I am a thousand winds that blow.
>
> I am the swift uplifting rush
> Of quiet birds in circled flight.
> I am the soft stars that shine at night.
> Do not stand at my grave and cry;

I am not there. I did not die.

Good luck to you all, and God bless!

References:

1. (Ghosts Among Us), James Van Praagh. August 2014.
2. Spirit, Man, Jinn by Ahmed Hulusi (Chapter 5-The Human Spirit).
3. http://www.merriam-webster.com/dictionary/koran.
4. (The Paranormal Dictionary) Chad L. Stambaugh page 50-51.
5. http://chatabout.com/topic/apparitions/top.
6. (The Soul After Death – Fr. Seraphim Rose.
7. Free Online Dictionary, Thesaurus and Encyclopedia.
8. (Death and the Afterlife: A Cultural Encyclopedia, Richard P. Taylor, 2000.
9. The Opening of the Mouth Ritual, Marie Parsons.
10. Social Studies School Service, Ancient Greece, 2003, page 49-51.
11. Bond, Jon 2004-06-13. Unitarians: Unitarian view of the afterlife. Retrieved 2014-03-08.
12. Searching for Spiritual Unity-Can There Be Common Ground? Page 582, Robyn E. Lebron-2012.
13. "Afterlife" Emanuel Swedenborg page 29.
14. "Harry Potter and the Sorcerer's Stone" J.K. Rowling.
15. (St. Martin Press, 1991) ISBN 0-312-06493-4.
16. From the Movie – (The Wolf Man), Curt Siodmak, 1941.
17. Wikipedia, the Free Encyclopedia – Supernatural and Paranormal.
18. (Merging Dimensions: The Opening Portals of Sedona) Tom Dongo and Linda Bradshaw, 1995.
19. Wikipedia, The Free Encyclopedia, Bennington Triangle.
20. "The Bennington Triangle" Weird encyclopedia.com" Frye, Todd (2007).
21. "The Vanished Town Of Glastenbury and The Bennington Triangle" by Chad Abramovich posted April 7, 2015.
22. (Associated Press) "E.V.W. Jones AP article" (http::/www.physics.smu.edu/pseudo/Bermuda Triangle/evwjones.html) Retrieved 1 October 2014.
23. "USCG: Frequently Asked Questions"(http://www.history.navy.mil/faqs/faq8-1htm) Uscg.mil.2008-07-22. Retrieved 20 November 2012.

24. "The Gulf Stream" Pamela Phillips, USNA/John Hopkins. Retrieved 2007-08-02.
25. "Bermuda Triangle: True Stories: Paranormal Mysteries" Graham Willcott. August 2015.
26. "Ecclesiastes 12:7.
27. "Ecclesiastes 3:20.
28. "Death and the Afterlife" Lynne Rudder Baker, 367.
29. "Death and the Afterlife" Lynne Rudder Baker, Introduction.
30. "Rev. 21-22"
31. "Rev. 20:11-15"
32. "Do Not Stand At My Grave And Weep" poem by MaryElizabeth.
33. Wikipedia, s.v. "Bigfoot".
34. Luke 1:41.
35. Ecclesiastes 9:5.
36. Wolfson 1956-57,8.
37. "Life On The Other Side" (Sylvia Browne, New American Library, 2000, Chapter 1).

Printed in the United States
By Bookmasters